AMERICAN INDIAN LEADERS TODAY

Dona Herweck Rice

Reader Consultants

Cheryl Norman Lane, M.A.Ed.
Classroom Teacher
Chino Valley Unified School District

Jennifer M. Lopez, M.S.Ed., NBCT
Teacher Specialist—History/Social Studies
Norfolk Public Schools

iCivics Consultants

Emma Humphries, Ph.D.
Chief Education Officer

Taylor Davis, M.T.
Director of Curriculum and Content

Natacha Scott, MAT
Director of Educator Engagement

Publishing Credits

Rachelle Cracchiolo, M.S.Ed., *Publisher*
Emily R. Smith, M.A.Ed., *VP of Content Development*
Véronique Bos, *Creative Director*
Dani Neiley, *Associate Content Specialist*
Fabiola Sepulveda, *Series Designer*

Image Credits: front cover Chip Somodevilla/Getty Images; p.4 Library of Congress [LC-USZC4-8937]; p.5 Joe Sohm/Visions of America/Universal Images Group via Getty Images; pp.6–9 Felia Hanakata; p.10 Carolyn DeMeritt; p.11 Alex Holder/Alamy; p.12 White House/SIPA/Newscom; p.13 USDA Photo by Bob Nichols; p.14 Marek Kasula/Alamy; p.15 Library of Congress [LC-DIG-ppmsca-12913]; p.16 Bettman/Getty Images; p.17 Paul J. Richards/AFP via Getty Images; p.18 Peter Rae/Fairfax Media via Getty Images; p.19 Bryan Smith/Zuma Press/Newscom; p.20 AP Photo; p.21 Granger Academic; p.22 AP Photo/Craig Ruttle; p.23 Rodin Eckenroth / Contributor Getty Images; p.24 Jacob Kepler/Bloomberg via Getty Images; p.25 (top) Angel Wynn/Danita Delimont/Newscom; p.25 (bottom) courtesy of The Mohegan Tribe; p.26 (bottom) Angel Wynn/Danita Delimont/Newscom; p.27 (top) Brian Cahn/Zuma Press/Newscom; p.29 Library of Congress [LC-DIG-highsm-12698]; all other images from iStock.

Shown on the cover are Hartford "Sonny" Black Eagle, Mary Black Eagle, and President Barack Obama.

Library of Congress Cataloging-in-Publication Data

Names: Rice, Dona, author.
Title: Tribal leaders / Dona Herweck Rice.
Description: Huntington Beach, CA : TCM, Teacher Created Materials, [2021].
| Includes index. | Audience: Grades 2-3 | Summary: "American Indian tradition is a rich and important part of American culture. Preserving tradition and culture is not always easy. Great leaders work to help preserve the important parts of history. They help to maintain fairness. And they lead communities into a bright and just future"-- Provided by publisher.
Identifiers: LCCN 2020016321 (print) | LCCN 2020016322 (ebook) | ISBN 9781087605111 (paperback) | ISBN 9781087619354 (ebook)
Subjects: LCSH: Indians of North America--Kings and rulers--Biography--Juvenile literature.
Classification: LCC E89 .R53 2021 (print) | LCC E89 (ebook) | DDC 970.004/97--dc23
LC record available at https://lccn.loc.gov/2020016321
LC ebook record available at https://lccn.loc.gov/2020016322

5482 Argosy Avenue
Huntington Beach, CA 92649-1039
www.tcmpub.com

ISBN 978-1-0876-0511-1
© 2022 Teacher Created Materials, Inc.

The name "iCivics" and the iCivics logo are registered trademarks of iCivics, Inc.
Printed in China
WaiMan

Table of Contents

Leaders and Legacies

Great leaders inspire. They teach. They show the way toward growth and advancement. The best leaders use the teachings of the past to move into a brighter future.

Today's American Indian leaders do all these things. They honor traditions. And they help find ways for the traditions to grow and bloom. They lead and guide the **Nations** into the best outcomes for modern life. They make sure that the **legacies** of the past are honored. And they make sure that modern Nations are treated with justice and respect.

American Indian leaders in the past

Meet some of today's American Indian leaders. Learn what they are doing to keep the Nations strong. See them inspire, teach, and help the Nations grow.

American Indian leaders today dressed in traditional clothes for a special event

Different Names

A *tribe* is a group of people who live near one another and have a common culture. A *clan* is a group who has shared ancestry. There can be many clans within a tribe. The term *tribe* most likely came from European settlers. Some American Indian groups prefer the term *Nation* to *tribe*.

Jump into Fiction

WILL REMEMBERS

"Do I have to go?" Will looked up from his game console, annoyed.

"*Have* to? No, you *get* to, Will." Dad stood in front of Will, his fringed and beaded garments in hand. Will's sister Lily stood next to her dad, her braided hair hanging down her back. She wore the colorful dress covered in jingles their grandma had made. And there stood Grandma at the kitchen door, holding a plate of freshly cooked fry bread—and looking disappointed in him.

"Okay, okay, Dad. I'm coming," Will said, just a little ashamed.

When he was younger, he thought these tribal outings were exciting, but all this tradition could wear a guy out. Why did he always have to go?

The family was a little late arriving at the field, and Will could hear the pulsing drum beat all the way down the road. He couldn't help but smile. Grandma winked and handed him a piece of fry bread as he got out of the car. Lily ran ahead to join her dance group, and Dad put his hand on Will's shoulder.

In the distance, they could see the tribal dancers moving to the beat of the drums. The singers' voices matched the rhythm and picked up the pace with the escalating energy of the dancers. Will felt the drumbeat like his own heartbeat. As they walked toward the powwow, Will remembered. "This is who we are," he said softly.

Dad squeezed his shoulder a little tighter and said aloud, "Yes, it is, Will. Always." And together they walked onto the field.

They were home.

Back to Nonfiction

Eddie Tullis: Leader

When Eddie Tullis was young, he had to take a bus 16 miles (26 kilometers) to get to school. Most of his day was spent going to school, learning, and coming home. When Tullis grew up, he wanted to make sure everyone had access to good local schools. Schooling is important to Tullis. One of the things he is most proud of is the focus on school among Poarch Creek Indians. He knows that one person's education can change the lives of many. He works with other leaders to be sure that Poarch Creek children are taught well.

Through the years, Tullis has also held many important roles. He has served at both local and national levels. He has been named to councils. He has served on committees. He has been a **mentor** and a leader at home. He has been a mentor and leader throughout the country as well.

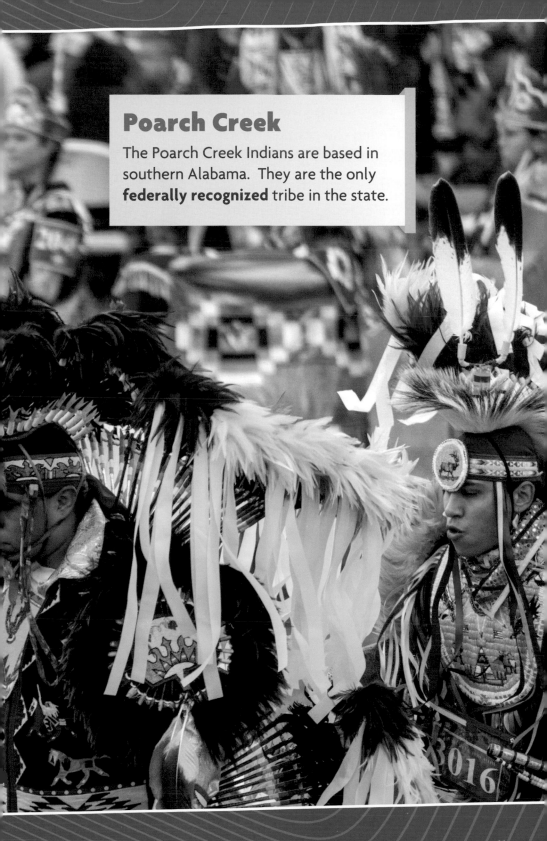

Poarch Creek

The Poarch Creek Indians are based in southern Alabama. They are the only **federally recognized** tribe in the state.

Tullis has served on the tribal council for the Poarch Creek Indians for years. He led the council for many of those years. He is a big reason why the Poarch Band of Creek Indians is recognized by the U.S. government. This happened less than 40 years ago. Of course, the tribe has existed much longer. They had to fight long and hard to be seen.

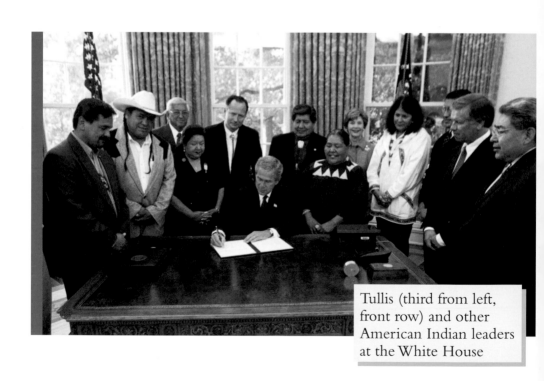

Tullis (third from left, front row) and other American Indian leaders at the White House

Tullis is a key reason why his tribe succeeds. He helps to make small and large changes. He works with other leaders to make changes happen. Tullis makes sure people follow laws too.

Tullis also records the history of the Poarch Creek Indians. In this way, he ensures that the stories of his people live on.

Doing Her Part

Like Tullis, Jayne Fawcett works to **preserve** American Indian culture. She has her own past to thank for her interest in the topic. Fawcett's family runs the oldest Indian-owned museum in the country.

Wilma Mankiller: Chief

Wilma Mankiller made history. She was the first modern female **principal chief** of a major tribe. That tribe is the Cherokee Nation.

Mankiller has been fighting for justice her whole life. She first worked as a **community organizer**. She helped people have a voice. She fought for fairness. She studied **treaty** rights. She helped the Cherokee Nation find ways to provide for itself too.

These wax figures honor historical Cherokee chiefs.

Then, Mankiller was in a very bad accident. She nearly died. It took her a long time to heal. But the fight for her life made her even more passionate. She was even more eager to help her people survive and succeed.

The Meaning Behind Mankiller

Mankiller says her family name has special meaning. It was given to people who watched over their villages. Those people were warriors.

Mankiller says that Cherokee people rely on one another. She learned a great deal from others about how people can work together for the good of all. She has kept and used these lessons all her life.

In time, Mankiller gained an interest in preserving old communities like her own. She wrote an essay about this topic. It came to the attention of the Cherokee principal chief at the time—Ross Swimmer. He liked what she had to say. He asked her to be his **deputy** in 1983. When he stepped down, Mankiller became principal chief. Some Cherokee people did not like it. They did not think a woman could do the job. She proved them wrong. In fact, she shined. She was elected on her own two more times. The work she did for the Cherokee Nation stands as a model for others.

As a tribal leader, Mankiller meets with President Ronald Reagan (seated to her right). A tribal leader is an elected official.

Mankiller with
President Clinton

Mankiller's Medal

The Presidential Medal of Freedom is a great honor.
It is given to someone who has made a major
contribution to the world. President Bill Clinton
awarded Mankiller this medal for her great work.

Oren Lyons: Changemaker

Oren Lyons is a faithkeeper. His job is to stay calm. He keeps the peace even when his people are in trouble. Lyons belongs to the turtle clan of the Onondaga Nation. It is one of the six Nations of the Iroquois (EER-uh-koy) confederacy. Lyons is a leader among his people. In fact, he works with **native** people around the world. His impact is huge.

As a young man, Lyons was a star athlete. He played lacrosse. He calls the game part of the "lifeblood" of the six Nations. Playing lacrosse is a **ceremonial** practice for his people.

After college, Lyons became an artist. He had a great career in New York. People celebrated his art. But members of his clan asked him to come home. They needed him to work for the good of the Nation.

Lyons and an Onondaga clan mother

Love of Lacrosse

Lyons was part of a special lacrosse team. It is made of Iroquois players from around the world. They compete in the world lacrosse championships each year.

Lyons (center) with the Iroquois Nationals lacrosse team in 2010

Lyons saw the need to protect the rights of his people. He convinced peace groups to speak at events about American Indian rights. These rights had often been overlooked. But more and more people spoke up. They wanted a change. Lyons led the way. He even went with other leaders to speak to the **United Nations**. He made them listen to what he had to say.

Lyons speaks about rights in 1974.

Iroquois leaders around 1570 meet to decide their laws.

Lyons saw that few U.S. leaders knew Iroquois history. Most leaders did not know the role his people played in forming the U.S. Constitution. Big parts of the Constitution were based on Iroquois practices. Lyons spoke to these leaders. In the end, they agreed with him. Congress made an official announcement. It said the Iroquois people played a key role in shaping the nation. Now, no one would forget.

Lyons also cares for the environment. He works hard to protect it. He works closely with Swedish leaders. They have joined forces to care for the world.

Lyons also works with leaders from many other faiths. He thinks such leaders can work together to heal and protect the world. His thinks the first step is to teach people to "be thankful for what [they] have and enjoy life."

Lyons speaks to people around the world about issues that matter to him. He tells people to take care of their families. He talks about how we all have to care for our environment. He defends human rights too. When Lyons speaks, he often includes this message: "You can't **negotiate** with a beetle." He believes that the laws of nature cannot be changed. It is up to people to change.

Lyons (center) marches in a 2014 protest.

Gay Kingman: Teacher

Gay Kingman was born to a family with strong ties to its past. History mattered to them. It matters to Kingman too. She is part of the Cheyenne River Sioux (SOO) tribe. This tribe is part of the Lakota Nation.

As a young woman, Kingman became a teacher. Teaching is her passion. She worked in schools for 25 years. She works to help all students succeed.

After teaching for years, Kingman's "classroom" grew. She was asked to take on a new role. She joined the Department of Education. There, she focused on equal rights for native students.

Kingman speaks to tribal leaders in 2009.

Lakota boys skateboard on a reservation.

Next, she became the head of the National Indian Education Association. She fought for better schools for native children. She spoke before Congress to get its support. She taught those leaders what needed to be done!

Chief Malerba

In 2010, Marilynn Malerba became the first modern female chief of the Mohegan Tribe. This tribe is based in the Northeast. Her mother plays an important role in the tribe as well. She is Tribal Nonner. This means an "elder female of respect."

Over time, Kingman worked with many leaders. They improved life for all tribal members. For example, some tribes have struggled to have enough money. Resorts and **gaming** have changed things. Through it, members of tribes find jobs. The tribes make money too. It can support whole communities. Kingman and others wanted to make sure that money earned from resorts and gaming staying on the **reservations**. They stood up for the rights of the native people.

The Lakota Nation operates this gaming establishment.

These modern–day tribal members meet for yearly events wearing traditional clothing.

Kingman got a job with the National Indian Gaming Association. That group is in charge of gaming. Kingman worked for its public relations (PR) team. A person who works in PR acts as a bridge between a company or group and the public. Kingman used PR to make sure that gaming helps tribes. She won major awards for her PR work.

Tribal Chairman

Kingman is now the director of the Great Plains Tribal Chairmen's Association. The goal of this group is to help different tribes work together. Her job means she is a key part of making this goal happen.

Leaders of Tomorrow

Today's tribal leaders have learned from the past. Now, they work for the future. They rely on the people who came before them. The leaders of tomorrow will continue today's work, and they will discover work of their own.

Each new leader stands on the shoulders of those who have gone before. This passing on of wisdom is an important part of tribal tradition. It has always been important. And it will continue to be so as new leaders move forward. As they do, bright tomorrows are sure to dawn.

a modern powwow in Virginia

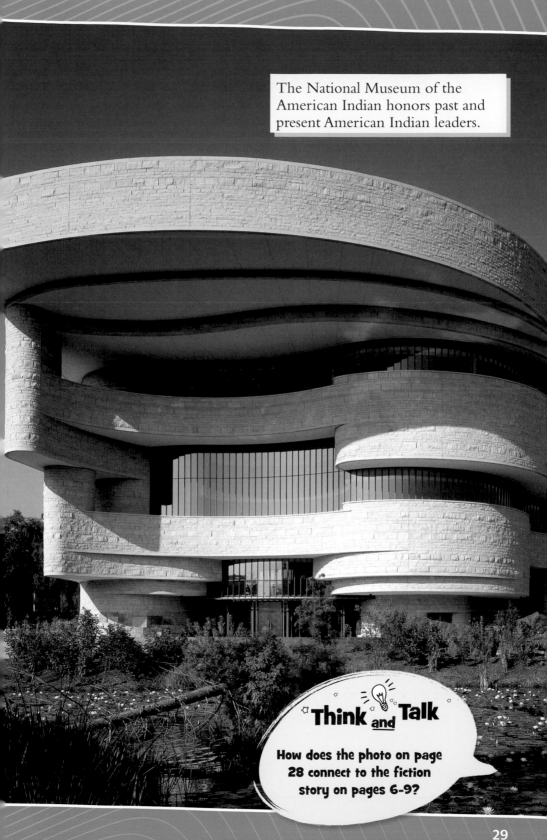

The National Museum of the American Indian honors past and present American Indian leaders.

Think and Talk

How does the photo on page 28 connect to the fiction story on pages 6-9?

Glossary

ceremonial—related to ceremonies and rituals

community organizer—a person who empowers people to work for the good of their communities

deputy—an assistant to the leader of a group

federally recognized—a tribe the U.S. government regards as having its own government

gaming—gambling; the practice of risking money in a game or bet

legacies—things from the past that have been preserved for the present

mentor—an advisor

Nations—tribes or groups of tribes that share history, traditions, and languages

native—a group of people who were already living in an area when other people arrived

negotiate—discuss a topic to find an agreement

preserve—keep something in good condition for future generations

principal chief—the title given to the leader of certain American Indian Nations and tribes

reservations—areas of land in the United States that are kept as separate places for American Indians to live

treaty—an agreement made between two or more groups or countries

United Nations—a group that works to increase cooperation between world governments

Index

Civics in Action

People can work with government leaders to make change happen. If someone has an idea on how to improve things, they can take on a leadership role. They can work with others to put their plan into action. They will develop and improve their leadership traits. Those traits can influence others too!

1. Think about your own traits.

2. Consider how those traits would make you a good leader.

3. Write a resume or fill out a job application as if you wanted to work with government leaders. Explain what you want to do and why you want to do it. Describe the traits you have that will help.